RECKONER

Wesleyan Poetry

RECKONER

James Tate

 Wesleyan University Press
Middletown, Connecticut

Some of the poems in this book appeared originally in these magazines: *The American Poetry Review, The Black Warrior Review, Crazy Horse, The Denver Quarterly, Durak, Iron Mountain Press Broadside, Kayak, The Massachusetts Review, The Milk Quarterly, The Missouri Review, Ploughshares, Poetry Australia, Poetry Miscellany, Poetry Now, Tendril,* and *Zero.*

The quoted epigraphs are used by permission of the publishers: Wallace Stevens, "The Man on the Dump," from *Collected Poems of Wallace Stevens,* copyright © 1954 by Wallace Stevens, Alfred A. Knopf, Inc.; W. H. Auden, "The Love Feast," from *Collected Shorter Poems, 1927–1957,* Edward Mendelson, ed., copyright © 1966 by W. H. Auden, Vintage Books, Random House Inc.; François Villon, "Ballade," Galway Kinnell, trans., from *The Poems of François Villon,* copyright © 1965, 1977 by Galway Kinnell, Houghton Mifflin Company.

The photograph opposite the title page is from Norman F. Carver, Jr.'s *Italian Hilltowns* and is used with his permission.

Library of Congress Cataloging-in-Publication Data

Tate, James, 1943–
   Reckoner.
   (Wesleyan poetry)
   I. Title. II. Series.
PS3570.A8R4 1986   811'.54   85-29550
ISBN 0-8195-5152-X (alk. paper)
ISBN 0-8195-6159-2 (pbk. : alk. paper)

All inquiries and permissions requests should be addressed to the Publisher, Wesleyan University Press, 110 Mt. Vernon Street, Middletown, Connecticut 06457.

Distributed by Harper & Row Publishers, Keystone Industrial Park, Scranton, Pennsylvania 18512.

Manufactured in the United States of America

FIRST EDITION

Wesleyan Poetry

For Liselotte

> Is it peace,
> Is it a philosopher's honeymoon, one finds
> On the dump? Is it to sit among mattresses of the dead,
> Bottles, pots, shoes and grass and murmur *aptest eve:*
> Is it to hear the blatter of grackles and say
> *Invisible priest;* is it to eject, to pull
> The day to pieces and cry *stanza my stone?*
> Where was it one first heard of the truth? The the.
>
> —Wallace Stevens, *"The Man on the Dump"*

Contents

I

Jo Jo's Fireworks—
Next Exit

Past the turpentine camps,
brilliant green lamps held
by woozy militiamen,
the car with a nose of its own,
with headlight-eyes, sniffs
through the mountain fog,
heart palpitating, belly
hungry for gasoline pancakes.
Ghettos rave in their sleep,
butchering alto solos,
harvesting white snakes.
The car, evermore threadbare,
feels lost on Chevrolet Avenue,
a victim of the Taxi Wars.
Salamanders glow like tiny cutlets
and each Inn is in secret
a detention barracks, each
exit an entrance to underground
cuniculi, concatenation
of clandestine suburbs
from which there is no escape
until dawn, when bellboys are young.

Stella Maris

There was nothing to do on the island. The dogs chased glass lizards into the dense myrtle bush. I don't know how the children slept. Men and women did what they could to extinguish the brightness of the stars.

One night my own supply of rum ran out, and I paced the verandah of my little hut-on-stilts. A ship was passing, the air was warm and moist like an animal's tongue. The island had once been home to pirates and runaway slaves, and giant sea turtles that crawled out by moonlight to lay their eggs. I no longer remembered what brought me there. And always the sound of the sea, like an overtone of eerie applause, the clapping of the palms of the palmettos.

I was dreaming, slightly intoxicated, and I found myself standing outside the little Catholic church, Stella Maris, "Star of the Sea." The priest stood before me, a beaten, disheveled man with ashes on his robes and the unmistakable aroma of alcohol like an unholy ghost drawing us closer.

"These people," he said, waving his arm around at his imaginary flock, "they think love's easy, something nice and tidy that can be bought, that makes them feel good about themselves. Believe me, it's a horrible thing to love. Love is a *terrible* thing, terrible!"

And I, an unbeliever, believed him. The next day the owner of the liquor store told me that the priest had been a Jew and a lawyer from New York before converting and becoming a priest assigned to this, the dregs of the Pope's Empire. Sharks and wild boar had thinned out the unbelievers. And Father Moser drank through the night, testing his faith with Fyodor Dostoevsky.

I never knew whether or not I had dreamed up that black-hearted priest, but I left the island shortly, and only now look back at my darkest hour with nostalgia.

The Planet of Rough Edges

I should attempt a short hill in the range of Bertha's Pain,
a climb designed to betray the view from too far behind. My
tail quickens, and I'm more like a carpenter inside his own
crate. I don't mind this rule of touching and smiling like
nails. Intruding into my inner-life, the day of rich gloam,
courageous breeding techniques preoccupied the rainforest, no.

There's a sorriness afloat here, around the streetcorner shops
with their sagging hearts: Pardon my palaverous welcome but
our last meeting slid by like a greased perch fingered in a
loud uncomfortable lounge. Adios, Toledo, see you in Ohio,
I whimpered but you didn't notice. Dear Mr. Shane and Simon
Moonbird too, this trying can be very trying, this essential

of which there are so many. It was a sad day in the hotdog
mortuary, ghost of Spring rain, O boo! We mopped up all
the blind stabs, not frightened about the days and the
strange feeble pride that makes excuses of their excuses.
I am speaking of the concealed staircase and the arc of years
which bloom; and everything else is sleeping in its prison,

your soul. I'm bent over that mystery, I fall free-fall
into the snowy wings, I breathe and destroy the noon
to escape the valley of my lone being.

Cleaning the Streets

I didn't know you were dead, I didn't know you could die.
I came out of the building, as usual. A pigeon flew into a Subaru.
A trolley zipped by at a thousand miles an hour. I had wanted to be
home for the news. Nearly everyone was falling down in the streets.
　　I thought back on the wisdom I had accumulated in Graduate
School: Is it appropriate for a junior executive to French kiss
a janitor? Should an aspiring cadet really contemplate suicide
on a regular basis? I was looking toward a sunset, appealing in its
boldness, over a modest lawn. My building was shrinking. I knew
I had to get home before the world stopped. I didn't know you were
dead.
　　I came out of the building, as usual. I reflected on my day:
a pigeon flew into a Subaru, and I was calculating the effect of this
on my Japanese neighbors, when I thought of my lost childhood.
　　I don't know much about public transportation.
　　I basketball within the swimming bicycle of our dimensions.
　　Like a kerchief blown to me from abroad,
　　like a kerchief in flames, I mean
　　to participate. Couldn't even find
　　the bus schedule, the eventual mugger
　　just when you need him, he is there, like
　　Christ I am feeling so much better
　　since I caught a popular disease.
　　I am helping clean the streets
　　of the most obviously dead.

No Rest for the Gambler

I am sitting quietly on the verandah, an instrument
for the composition of replies is smoking next to me,
a decoy with a frown.

These are the kinds of details that exhaust me—pine
needles, a fly in a web, seashells—the details
you can never forget for noticing—Sophia's slowly

gliding ducks, her cleavage, her gum. . . . I have questions
that take the form of whippings with fronds, of idleness,
unhappy ancestors fanning the dawn. I predict the destruction

of the temples of Hucumba, and the election of Slick Jones.
Something once terribly important has been lost,
like an island, an embroidered blouse, a colleague

in the parallel world. A swindler's victory, a fly
I had once known. I disapprove, I don't remember!
Beyond the reef are sharks and the dainty frippery

of childhood, and, once there, there is no filching.
I was premature on the beach, like algae at lunchtime
sleepwalking with a harp proscribed by hawks.

One looks backward and one looks forward.
Dust is watching life's talk show.
I plunge like danger into the sea.

My mother stands, facing the wind.

The Pyramids,
Once Disrobed

The pyramids, once disrobed, reverberate
with travesties, are whisked off
for urine samples and loamy cloaks.

The wet mossy areas are examined
by rubbergloves. The gloves ogle
unprofessionally the brooding mounds,

and the pink clouds drip noiselessly above.
Let's see if I can dislodge this eyelid
from the formaldehyde, and slither

this intoxicating zinc patter over to the foxglove
docks before midnight when the vanquished
from the savanna return with their bulldogs.

My hatpin has turned to ash and then
to some sort of larva which insists
on climbing the staircase out of here,

however morosely, however bitten
and coveted by our pet prowler.
And the pyramids puff and occasionally swoon

when I pinch them or poke them with the dust mop.
Hesitation cherished a fragrant curve.
And this seems to soothe them: a breast, a hatpin.

On the Shores
of Lake Disappointment

Lumbering, carnal meditations. Fleet, mystic revelations. Beautiful, guilty dirges. All with scared, immigrant eyes, all seeking the key. The barnstorming preacher, the vendor of homeopathies, the landlord and butcher, the graduate student—all look down the road to the same truth: The doors of the major publishing houses are closed to them.

One step from home the restless wind was put away in its carved box. Children stand there knee-deep in dead leaves waiting for something else to come along. You can't convince them things were ever different, trusting, as they do, only in Martians.

Tell a green man something—

He was made of money *and* he grew on trees.

An invitation arrives: "Here is an opportunity to meet people exactly like yourself. . . ." My handkerchief jumps out of my pocket and daubs blood on my trembling hands.

We'll Burn That Bridge
When We Come to It

Silhouette of my hieroglyph,
hyena of my foibles,
and even puniness of my astrological endeavor,
I am scolding these shabby shipmates.
One of them can sneer and sing in falsetto
while murdering frogs—he's a green blowfly
not worthy of scratching our curiosity.
Another left the waterworks for a monastery
in an indigo field, terminating
his little income from the face of the earth.
And there I am, a million tons of buffalo bones,
reconnoitering the chalky goldfields,
raven in hand, grunting imperial sulphur belches
beside the wagon where her blouse hangs
in opalescent darkness, grievous spasms.

O abstinence of my corpulent debauches,
and satchel of my chanting,
turbulence of my decimated bandana,
I am celebrating all this forlorn gazing:
the ship stiffens, numbed by an impulse to fly.

My Nephew's Hotels

His lynx eyes fidgeting
with his internal beret,
my nephew promises to plant
an evergreen somewhere
for all of us, and a speedy
trial for the jurors.
But Polly wants her chocolate almonds
when the vice squad knocks
on his door at 4 A.M.
Suddenly there is an enraged boulevard
blinking, which wasn't there before,
and the Captain says, "Oh,
what the hell, let's call
room service for pancakes."
My nephew weeps, *I am chained to my hotels!*

My nephew's hotels are built on cliffs
all over the world. They maintain
a certain standard—mean, dirty, always
begging for more. Like a pistol beneath
a pillow, always begging for more.

Detained

Savoring drowsiness
to a muffled calculation,
I probe with my encrusted tool
bringing violets to a sawmill.
This is a prophet in tweeds,
a cordial rebel on a spree
puckered like an almanac
for the decisive detail: shoe polish
that falls from a shelf at nightfall,
tentacles around a horse,
a flowerpot with toothpicks growing in it,
an ankle wrapped in gauze,
a church full of bananas,
gilt sandbags. I trace
this ribbon of scent to its origin
or to where I am detained
outside the castle walls.

Jelka Revisited

Jelka's profile decorates the doorway to my secret architecture.
Jelka's profile chaffs at its own imposture, and the indirection
of its stardust infiltrates my polar brain: Welcome
to the material world where omens of the afterworld are leaked,
flowing like a black shirt. Mountains migrate into my head:
I was there to witness the vulgar radiance of her method,
dimly brooding under my Western lamp, accustomed, as I am,
to a miscellany of risible phantasms, fatigue never set in.
"Pungent nit, come in! Comfort my belligerent lashes, help me
cast out my throes." Jelka's profile, O the asymmetry of it all!
She staggers now, and attempts to install a puzzle in her smile.
To the tune of Gylfi's mocking, this goddess of illusion
I shall never forget: all living is forgiving. Her profile.

Within Jelka's radius, a Colonel is pulling a thorn
from a comrade's melancholy frown.
There is undischarged thunder in the air. Skeptical,
Jelka looks around, spots a mathematician
playing marbles in the darkened parlor.
Several travelers appear indisposed and refuse
an offer of dinner. Jelka is stimulated
by these companions and walks around
feeling pregnant. Was Hirshvogel going North
or South? "Go after him when you are bigger,"
said the neighbor. The buttons, the buttonholes,
silver heels—brooch which consists of single
flaming beryl—whisk broom, please, carhop. The fête
by the tomb was a horrible idea. Jelka's tongue
felt like suede. Her slippers, too, were antique, blessed things
making sure she "never fell off Mister Floor."

Thirty olive trees are scribbling with crayons
on the bowler hats of eagles—ah, the train!
Jelka snatched up the idle boy, the viscous child saint,
and cuddled him all the way to Illinios.
Wanderers. Whoosh, their luggage. They stand there,
pigheaded in Poisonville, bleeding lemonade
onto the drip-dry tarmac. They are traveling
under pseudonyms, their whole lives flickering
in corridors. Around five, the bonfires,
and they come whipcracking out of their comas.
Lynxes are burrowing into their sleep-filled wagons.
And the boy with the mark of the beast . . . his
transitory gleam and headlong flight . . . Jelka follows
him flattening her endearments against the linoleum
shadow-stippled in the afternoon.

Jelka was lost forever, her costume found burnt
at daybreak. Could have been the city itself
just having a good time. I wish I knew
its name, brute nebulae. When her Collected Phonecalls
were published last Fall, she didn't remember
making any of them. So. American roués.
She was a ghost at her own birthday party.
"Look at her," said the Colonel, "she twiddles the dust-babies,
baleful and bluish, with fewer fingernails to grow.
Her life swings back and forth like a tongueless bell,
so far from anyone's home." I wrung his neck, and now
all of that old world is torn down. A coach arrives
to take her back to her inkspot, her comfortable

decomposing zones.

A Beer Ain't Got
No Bone

I can't pick up the vacuum cleaner
without remembering our most subtle
and tender moments, shooing the sniper
from the playground, then picking watermelons.
For the past few months my life has read
like canned-food labels caked with panic.
I don't know if she's still in Tokyo
or on her way to Zanzibar. I am throwing
snowballs at the roadmap, I have placed
a thumbtack in the bluish hideaway
of her portrait.

              I wonder if she thinks
about me at all. As I lie in bed dreaming
about her, a mouse is playing with a model airplane.
I could see the resemblance to her disorder;
in a downpour of thistles I could not forget her,
her absence lashed! My wife desisted,
an amphibian pulling anchor. Home,
the piddling copper tubing, the soap,
the grapefruit asks about her.
The syrup and ice trays have asked about her.
Without her, the cabaret is not so rosy,
falters before the greenery of life.

Love Gets Ornery

I called her my untamable cupcake,
she was a humanoid in jodhpurs,
a jigsaw on the stage of the ballet,
We met in a tourist cabin near a famous crater.
Macaroni in leotards, I noted in my notebook.
She could prattle until the floodlights goo-ed her lollipop.
A sarcasm, fervent and amplified, that could stop a hurricane.

But it was all a charade: toward sundown, when love gets ornery,
a massive infusion of minor disputes dampened our zeal,
and motley decibels were squandered in teeny veering snaps.
Routed, I scraped the pulpit with my espionage trombone.
I called her my untamable cupcake and whispered goodbye.

People's Soupbones

Bones of a spotted leopard,
sad, anonymous bones.

A quiet cough, when the bones gleam,
this itsy-bitsy louse called fame.

The house rocks, and people stand
in doorways looking suspicious,

looking bones of a spotted leopard
in the face, the sure grace boiled down

to but the faintest broth.
People look into themselves,

see the Edens they have not
left room for. The famous bones

of the spotted leopard
are all they have.

II

Smart and
Final Iris

Pentagon code
for end of world
is *rural paradise,*
if plan fails
it's *rural paradise*

For losses under
100 million, *a trip
on the wayward bus*

For a future of mutants,
bridal parties collide

World famine is
a plague of beatniks

First strike and
*I sniff your nieces
I fall to pieces
Get hell out . . .*

A madman comes,
one of those babies
the further you kick it
the bigger it gets.

The Chaste Stranger

All the sexually active people in Westport
look so clean and certain, I wonder
if they're dead. Their lives are tennis
without end, the avocado-green Mercedes
waiting calm as you please. Perhaps it is
my brain that is unplugged, and these
shadow-people don't know how to drink
martinis anymore. They are suddenly and
mysteriously not in the least interested
in fornicating with strangers. Well,
there are a lot of unanswered questions
here, and certainly no dinner invitations
where a fella could probe Buffy's inner-
mush, a really complicated adventure,
in a 1930ish train station, outlandish
bouquets, a poisonous insect found
burrowing its way through the walls
of the special restaurant and into one
of her perfect nostrils—she was reading
Meetings with Remarkable Men, needing
succor, dreaming of a village near Bosnia,
when a clattering of carts broke her thoughts—
"Those billy goats and piglets, they are
all so ephemeral . . ." But now, in Westport
Connecticut, a boy, a young man really,
looking as if he had just come through
a carwash, and dressed for the kind of success
that made her girlfriends froth and lather,
can be overheard speaking to no one
in particular: "That *Paris Review* crowd,
I couldn't tell if they were bright or
just overbred." Whereupon Buffy swings
into action, pinning him to the floor:

"I will unglue your very being from this
planet, if ever . . ." He could appreciate
her sincerity, not to mention her spiffy togs.
Didymus the Blind has put three dollars
on Total Departure, and I am tired of pumping
my own gas. I'm Lewis your aluminum man, and
we are whirling in a spangled frenzy toward
a riddle and a doom—here's looking up

your old address.

Ash Manor

The ghost said nothing that added to our knowledge
of the current situation at Ash Manor, only, as he parted,
"Your flesh would make delicious veal chops
for hungry wolves." Then he called us his "disciples."

Like the slow emigration of the mad, in the half-silence,
I blew upon the lock of the door and it opened.
I blew upon the candle, which lit itself. It was not
a dream—it was a puzzle. In my mouth there was a bowl

of beef stew, but I could not eat it. I felt hungry,
but it was not really hunger, only a feeling of hunger.
Though, fortunately, observations on bees living in the tropics
have thrown a little light on the question: as if I had

bitten my throat with my own teeth. Nevertheless the waves
of the primeval Ocean of Tantalassa were swashing over
pet seals, Tex and Tulip. A Cult was immediately formed
whose solemn purpose it was to design new uniforms for the
    servants.

Here was a sad emotion, belonging exclusively to the sphere
of civilized man. Photographs were taken of a trumpet
in the air; a rebuke, it nested there long after sunset,
in darkness. My eyes moistened, my great burning eyes.

The dwarfs on my side were like myself, only much shorter
and black. The dwarfs on the other side were real dwarfs,
who were really six feet tall like myself, or even eight feet tall,
but they looked as if they were no bigger than a child.

I have a little dog and they want to take him away from me.

Machines are being installed in my head.

A Vagabond

A vagabond is a newcomer
in a heap of trouble.
He's an eyeball at a peephole
that should be electrocuted.
He's a leper in a textile mill
and likely to be beheaded, I mean,
given a liverwurst sandwich
on the break by the brook
where the loaves are sliced.
But he oughtn't meddle
with the powder puffs on the golf links—
they have their own goats to tame,
dirigibles to situate.
He can act like an imbecile
if the climate is propitious,
a magnate of kidnap
paradising around the oily depot,
or a speck from a distant nebula
wishing to purchase a certain skyscraper. . . .

Well, if it's permitted, then
let's regulate him, let's testify
against his thimble, and moderate his gloves
before they sew an apron.

The local minister is thinking
of moving to Holland, exchanging
his old ballads for some lingerie.
"Zatso!" says the vagabond.
Homeless, like wheat that tattletales
on the sermon, like wages swigged.
"Zatso, zatso, zatso!" cries the vagabond.
The minister reels under the weight
of his thumbs, the vagabond seems to have

jutted into his kernel, disturbed
his terminal core. Slowly, and with
trifling dignity, the minister removes
from his lapel his last campaign button:
Don't Mess with Raymond, New Hampshire.

Pigs of the Deep

I have tusks ablaze in a distant pavilion.
The orphaned streetcar is primping
outside the telegraph office
as if there were a ceasefire in her boudoir.
And I, a fledgling, chittering about
the recent massacres, come back as a traveler,
set sail as a sailor, throw up my hands as a merchant.
My snoring has awakened a moist spot in her, that is,
in her *Weltschermz,* a homesickness for a place
she has never been. My affliction claws

like an owl with veins of turquoise
on a streetcar named *Weltschmerz.*
The little pigs of the deep sea
come looking for me with searchlights
the size of buttons, on bicycles
made out of discarded scissors, ringing bells
that were stolen from the bakery, relics
away from home for the first time.

I'm a man, because I hold my own stem
which blushes like a sunflower,
because I plunge like a snake through honey
and shave with a babbling goldfish.
A man, looking more like a sycamore
cradling a crayfish, still more
like a triangle of porcelain
about to turn to cream. A man comes
sprinkling his shyness down the cherry staircase,
humming the same tune to which, only moments before,
the little pigs of the deep sea had been dancing.

He keeps a dead canary by the windowless curtains,
never disturbed by a sunbeam.

Who Is Jenny

Who is Jenny lying to
In her call, Collect, to Rome?
The Love that made her out of nothing
Tells me to go home.
   —W. H. Auden, "The Love Feast"

Jenny of the flatlands postcard skedaddle,
Jenny the patrician valedictorian that wiggles
and did her rendition of Rubberband Waterfall
while raunchy topics romped among the fruit flies.

*

Jenny, Jenny of the surveillance walkie-talkies,
and what about the drainboard and the clothesline, huh?
Jenny of the glade, of the inlet, of the shoals,
can she remember the hot sulphur springs?

*

On a sunny day our high-strung washing machine
keels over. Our genitals feel like chessmen stealing
hubcaps. We had hunkered down with the riffraff,
genteel cadavers ricocheting like sparks around a mandolin.

*

Whew! the hospitality seeping like a broadcast
ululating ninnies from the remnant of an infantry,
attuned to pointillist dandelions, made us feel
abdominal disenchantment, and immune, like spooks or ghouls.

*

Jenny is employed as a stenographer for the sorcerers' rodeo.
She sizzles with resentment at the masks they wear.
And I am straddling a mosaic in the tumult of her apparatus.
We divide a lean, lime-colored snakeskin.

28

The Little Sighs
Bite a Sheet

Every day someone walks into the local zoo
and saws off the head of a live moose, drifters
skin random poodles for no reason. I know

more about a certain *ménage à trois* than I
would like. We are here asking these questions,
I am writing this in the middle of nowhere,

coaxing myself into this embarrassing photograph
with ten thousand dolls I never met before.
Eighteen exploding possums covered with prayer rugs.

The quotidian melancholy lulls me into dreamless sleep.
Given the supposed diversity of life, the daring
post-parakeet rendezvous is made to parade because

I could detect the cross moss of a cello after
the last candle had withdrawn its nose from the world.
Everything's a dream when you're alone with the hollow

bones of a bird. His name is so familiar it's pathetic,
the riddle of his voice, where the deepest sighs congregate
to piss off the masters of the little sighs.

After the Theater

It is somewhat irresponsible
to saunter after the theater
through the nameless town
with the nameless congregation
as if nothing had transpired.

As if shrewdness could get you anywhere.

Go and catch a falling star: you don't
win anything with behavior like that.

Only the privileged newspaper writers
are sitting in their favorite café.
Cunning, on a small scale, kidnaps you
for the next half hour, streaking inade-
quacies across the front-page items—

the two size-nine bathing suits out on bail

have now masterminded the information daringly:
Sady Stralson's suspicions and complaints
                                        linger. . . .

                        *

Gramwell had calmed Henrietta enough
to make her agree to take a little rest;
but he had been careful to place her in a room
from which it was impossible to escape.
Thus it is easy, the plot said, to follow

a subject's destination, and to return without
honor at the hour of coma, momentum in disarray.

No, I come to you because you are a wonderful
and terrible antelope who chanted to a lady
in my presence. "Will you marry me?"

*

Not at all!

*

All through the years of the potato riots
we were absorbed in question-and-answer games.
The church records, grief-stricken, satisfied us.
Thus it is easy to forgive our conduct in the face
of such hindrances. If a message came, it was

secondhand, with errors consistently. Giodwad,
the shepherd, more than the other creatures, witnessed
"Ultimate Truths" in burial dates. "Baptism," he said,
"that's too easy. An instinct, after the theater,
is needed. A walk among the insolent creatures

not employed by the State."

The Commune's Storehouse
Is Bursting with Grain

Reading the communiqué stirred me deeply,
and I squeezed my bagpipes at harmless intervals,
and shuffled rapid-wavy-ducklike
outside among the nighttime fish scales.
Jumping frogs were bleeding on the sawdust.

Only the flickering lantern breathes in this scene with me,
and the cooing of sleepless molecules,
untamed antheaps snickering beneath me.
The moon goes thud into her niche.

This gives me pause to wonder at my progress,
the padlocks, nutcrackers and saucepans that ridicule,
the whips and talkative larvae waiting to ambush.
A ritual despair that empties in preparation for filling
the granaries simultaneously in several busted dimensions.

And in between I pry seething, radiant almonds
from my bagpipes.

Reading the communiqué must have stirred me deeply.

The Flithering Ignominy
of Baba Ganoosh

He played the bongo drums and dated infant actresses.
His signature still glitters in all the most exhausted hotels.
He has positive contempt for rain, for chattering.
His sofa was designed by a butcher.

You can read about my Baba Ganoosh: the newspapers
have memorized the shapelessness of his journey.
Peril, fatigue, peril, perplexity—he's on the move
in all the right nondescript shrubbery,

he really cushions the savage tubas of life.
He is the springboard to the shadowy, the sewer
of ashamed freight, a talking turtle.
Somehow he embodies all that shriveled future

where huddling in an abandoned garden with a last companion
will be unthinkable, like a paradise that blinks,
or frequently pushes the wrong button
and thinks thoughts like *barbed wire*.

The Inscrutable Cinema

In the lobby of the local cinema stood the nocturnal priest,
his eyes downcast. The movie was just beginning, a wagonload
of acrobats passed beyond the curtain, *A Fable of Looting*,
proclaimed the silvery poster. Documents would have to be
smuggled, delicious night trains derailed, windswept rockets
dislodged from the hypnotized participants.

The priest entered and disappeared into the audience, ready for
their confessions, his tomahawk and thermos of gin breaking laws
when he felt the need. On the screen the supreme villain spoke
confidentially of his childhood, and the priest wagged his head
up and down, and frowned into his demoralized quagmire. Then
who was left to do the looting but the brightest of all stars;
furtively, the night and all its acts were signed away,

the signature illegible.

Signs of Distress

There sat the Doctor in his swivel chair
staring into space with an eyeball in his forceps.
Evidently he was eating lunch, a plate of fried eel
and popcorn littered his desk, and next to the picture of his wife
was a sack of flour.

Two aging geese sat beneath his wall clock
whimpering about the pains in their necks.
A polar bear in sunglasses stood in the doorway
holding a penny by its edge.

Some mushrooms were growing by the telephone.
Suddenly, laughter gripped the Nurse.
The Doctor diagnosed a blister and stabbed lewdly
at her nose with his tweezers.

O the Hospital is completely out of thumbtacks
and logic and sausages and Eskimos.
The Hospital really needs some chilly noses
and another trillion miles of rope.
There are so many murky details that need
to be seen to, the cells and the sobs and the craving.

And why doesn't the Emergency Ward panic
and howl with all those tree stumps and broken circles?
The palpable intimacy of those collisions
requiring all that straw and mud to lull
the central shining nervous system. . . .

It is no wonder that the Doctor himself sometimes
identifies the victim as his enemy,
and can be heard playing his flute of illusion
futilely by the coiled railroad tracks
of his brief lunch,
and the Nurse shrieks beside herself to see such a sight.

Magazines

I've been feeling so cooped up in this hotel, room service so far I can't decipher. Are they really duds? I can't decipher. Because I like fussing with a wayward lamp, whisk broom, please. Now I know you're pulling my leg. So much figurine enchilada, umpteen laryngitis. My hardship is up against the prevailing voltage. As a tenant, I'm gullible. Oh, I see, it's the rheumatism that tarnished your hula, Room 309. Both parents were transvestites for the poor slob in 315? He had no . . . storage. There was no . . . umbrella. I came here on a whim, curious about Japanese. At a poolside tribute my mum's rumors were cancelled. At the anniversary of the plague, I caroused the rippling studio of my neighbor's ailment. Born in Singapore? You spilled some suds on my hoodlum friend. If you had a nickelodeon you wouldn't play it.

I'm feeling, how long does an earthworm live? Ten years. Like yesterday was bird dung. And you, the reader, are cheating, lifeless patches of celery. I ask these questions on cue, like a trauma victim. Could you summarize the twinkling visage that engulfed you at the bazaar? Room, an unforeseen passageway into a coyote's bordello after a long, sweet nightmare. And I had my chance, cradling a pet rabbit, smashing a pewter mug against my shinbone. When it comes to decoding bits of information from the trees, I'm a prevaricating modular dewlap, never heard of withershins or the Nutmeg State. Like you, I want to know the author.

Save the Mosquitoes

Just before dawn
the huge glass doors
of the pea-packing plant
are rolled back
and the mosquitoes
are filing their needles
and the inspector
straightens his eyebrows
and spanks them
for good luck.

Bewildered wall clocks continue
in their grinding poverty.
The birdcages are festooned:
for whom? An ancient kimono
is a kind of dead weight,
avoirdupois, typical of this
morning's saffron harvest.

The mosquitoes glitter over
the windswept platform
and swoop in loose formation
along some dotted lines.
The town is still puffed
from the night before,
TVs rippling in the dark.

A crane is paying a courtesy call
on a shrine. A small-craft warning
is flashed across the sky.
This plausible life, at the appointed hour,
is escorted across the midway, dazzled
by the vacuum of dawn
and its abiding bashful grace.

The Dead Man's Medicine

I think of the waves of friends, for it is true
they come and go in waves—the little ones gone
forever and so forth. Several pink hams must be
delivered immediately!

Then a white crocodile appears out of nowhere.
I feel the dread of being alone, and the dread
of being with people. Nothing comes naturally
to me now. Disappointing tomatoes lack interesting bugs.

What hurt may be within, or passed on to another,
as proof of anything, is a Martini when all
the birds have flown; or a breeze of maniacs
rotting serenely into the dependable noon.

What I like is Autumn, the sexiest season, mulch.
When the baked cranial seed-pasture is mystified
by love, and my handwriting explodes with freaky loops,
suicidal slopes, wind-worn ridges.

Soft curved thing, roach who insists on wearing mink,
Jaguar, it is your mountain, your skyscraper, green bean.
Soft curved thing, missile that carries love letters
to the enemy, marmalade of death, the empress herself

wants to see you. The empress herself has one desire,
to be ravished by the jaguar, to be ravished by the
empress herself has one desire. Soft curved thing,
it is your mountain, green bean. A hair's breadth,

very close—"Watch it, Bix—railroad crossing."—
a fingernail's astonishment at bronze, very close
to lifting the veil, the hospital gown. Tempest
and sunshine, very close. Some orphans are stricken

with typhoid, and that is going to blemish our jubilee.
Like gnawing on the finish line or broken rocks.
I have my own rags for special functions:
For ordeals in cafeterias I dress up like a wolverine.

In a long black coat, wearing a crew cut, comes
Mr. Merkle and Moonteeth the Wild Sow.

"Watch it—bump ahead," I cried.

III

There's no care except hunger
No favors but from an enemy
Nothing edible but a bale of hay
No lookout but there's a man asleep
No clemency without a crime
No safety but among the frightened
No good faith but a disbeliever's
Nor any cool heads but lovers.

—François Villon, "Ballade"

Neighbors

Will they have children? Will they have more children?
Exactly what is their position on dogs? Large or small?
Chained or running free? Is the wife smarter than the man?
Is she older? Will this cause problems down the line?
Will he be promoted? If not, will this cause marital stress?
Does his family approve of her, and vice versa? How do
they handle the whole inlaw situation? Is it causing some
discord already? If she goes back to work, can he fix
his own dinner? Is his endless working about the yard
and puttering with rain gutters really just a pretext
for avoiding the problems inside the house? Do they still
have sex? Do they satisfy one another? Would he like to
have more, would she? Can they talk about their problems?
In their most private fantasies, how would each of them
change their lives? And what do they think of us, as neighbors,
as people? They are certainly cordial to us, painfully
polite when we chance-encounter one another at the roadside
mailboxes—but then, like opposite magnets, we lunge backward,
back into our own deep root systems, darkness and lust
strangling any living thing to quench our thirst and nourish
our helplessly solitary lives. And we love our neighborhood
for giving us this precious opportunity, and we love our dogs,
our children, our husbands and wives. It's just all so damned
difficult!

The Sadness
of My Neighbors

Somehow, one expects
all that food
to rise up
out of the canning jars
and off the dinner plates
and *do* something,
mean something.

But, alas, it's all
just stuff and more
stuff, without pausing
for an interval
of transformation.

Even family
relationships
go begging
for any illumination.

And yet, there is competence,
there is some quiet
glitter to the surface,
a certain cleanliness,
which means next to

nothing, unless you want
to eat off the floor.

Thoughts While Reading
The Sand Reckoner

What nourishes the polar star?
That's a story I refuse to tell.
Bellhops lacking a pineapple?
Or the secret ingredients of bubblebath?
Itself a derailed story. And still
stuntmen by the school are washed ashore.
What would be inappropriate here is deep-
fried calamaries, or the sound of a crossbow
humming. I have been reading for hours,
I am counting every little grain of sand.
Saturday night in Amherst: Archimedes is my man.
I drift toward nightfall, renaming all
the recent immigrants from Antarctica.
("We shall have a good voyage if God is willing.")
Disconsolate bunglers, incalculable cloves,
the Ship sang. Ginger scurvy.
Then I took one of them around to see chlorophyll
working in the meadow, and later bought him
a porkpie hat. Night was coming on, hell,
night had come and gone and I was still
reading, reading my way through the library.
Night had come and gone leaving not a trace
except me, and I by necessity had moved on
and was by now reading *Magellan's Voyage,*
a Narrative Account of the first Circum-
navigation by Antonio Pigafetta. Poor mad
Ferdinand died spectacularly at the hands
of Filipino warriors. Seventeen hundred
years before a fellow named Eratosthenes
calculated the circumference of the earth
to be 24,650 miles—not a bad guess, only
two-hundred and twenty-five off. Well,
I was reading about all these stargazers
and felt this aching desire for a newer world

when *Adventures of a Red Sea Smuggler*
tumbled off the shelf. I love Henry de Monfreid
for writing, "I went to see the pyramids.
What a disappointment they were to me. . . ."
His reason: the majesty of the desert
could not be obscured.

Sunday morning in Amherst, I have spotted
a water buffalo! Emily Dickinson
has decided to purchase several mohair jackets,
but it is Sunday and I regret to report
she has not been a very good neighbor lately.
"Tears are my angels now," she said to me
around 4 A.M. "But are they interested
in Cedar Rapids?" I asked. "I'm not qualified
to say," was her sorry reply. And so it went,
the sound of a crossbow humming, my own
jungle fever. My weary and blossoming Soul
was passed from hand to hand to hand.
I was resting in the center of some huge pageant
when a human standing next to me said:
"There must be more," and set out to find it
against all odds, against the known sum.
And years later, either came back or didn't,
was the biggest fool ever, or shines there
on the horizon, like a newly minted coin of hope.
And those who stayed and mocked, and those
who merely read about it later—the grains
of untrammelled sand fall through their brains
long after the sojourner has begun to snore.

Storm

The snow visits us,
taking little bits of us with it,
to become part of the earth,
an early death and an early return—

like the filing of tax forms.
And all you can say after adding up
column after column: "I'm not myself."

And all you can say after the long night
of searching for one certain scrap of paper:
"It never existed."

And when all the lamps are lit
and the smell of the stew
has followed you upstairs
and slipped under the door of your study:
"The lute is telling the story
of the life I might have lived,
had I not—"

In my study, which is without heat,
in mid-January, in the hills
of a northern province—only
the thin white-haired volumes
of poetry speak, quietly, like
unfed birds on a night visit

to a cat farm. And an airplane is lost
in a storm of fitting pins.
The snow falls, far into the interior.

Short March,
Teeny Wall

A quarrel undresses
an impulse, textbooks
are deposited, but aroused.
A tyranny is subdued
while a rabbit examines

his poultry. Many dimensions
are motionless, like a flood
nowadays appeals to the
tiniest birchtrees. There's
a nuance there, palpable

as a railroad in the ozone
where civilians are debris,
autumnal wind battering
the curtains in the buildings.
My spine is humming music

sheets. My neck is in the door
beneath my eyes. My hand
is whore-hunting beside
the theologues in the church
of intrigue, of serpentine

deportations and imbroglios
mutually embedded in the blind
keyhole of our instruments.
Where the cloud is cleft,
and the machinery is suffocating,

a physician is departing, tush, tush.
An expedition of breathing animals
catapults the bank into bronze,
and the operations of my own personal
mechanism recognize the haziness

of boundaries, with deep respect.
I silence the bells at the doorway.
I call the boys home through thick vines
and fermentation of a national crisis.
In a white tuxedo, I am the bouncer in heaven.

Tuesday's Child Is:
Full of Grace

Too soon she is the grandmother,
able to live only for others,
when what she wants is to be left alone.
This one, Tuesday's child, it's not that
she wants to die, nor does she live
on memories. For her, the past exists
no more than the future. She waits
and watches the body decay, the eye
cease to observe. Tuesday's child
is full of grace. The Lord exists
in her eye, with his only chance for fame.

A Wedding

She was in terrible pain the whole day,
as she had been for months: a slipped disc,
and there is nothing more painful. She

herself was a nurse's aid, also a poet
just beginning to make a name for her
nom de plume. As with most things in life,

it happened when she was changing channels
on her television. The lucky man, on the other
hand, was smiling for the first time

in his life, and it was fake. He was
an aspiring philosopher of dubious potential,
very serious, but somehow lacking in

essential depth. He could have been
an adequate undertaker. It was not the first
time for either of them. It was a civil

service, with no music, few flowers.
Still, there was a slow and erratic tide
of champagne—corks shot clear into the trees.

And flashcubes, instant photos, some blurred
and some too revealing, cake slices that aren't
what they were meant to be. The bride slept

through much of it, and never did we figure out
who was on whose team. I think the groom
meant it in the end when he said, "We never

thought anyone would come." We were not the first
to arrive, nor the last to leave. Who knows,
it may all turn out for the best. And who

really cares about such special days, they
are not what we live for.

Holiday on an Antfarm

They danced like programmed angels.

In Nature's
most exclusive capitol
they danced
with domestic forethought.

I refuse to say anything dirty about them,
for mud is a fashion
not chosen by the wild ones.

Autochthonous

A man named Bates was monitoring our ways,
filled, as we were, with the red-purple sap
of this place. "Whup!" I growled with an undecided hop.
Little triangles of heaped-up moss astonished him,
while the torn glove he uncovered acted as a sedative.

Ostensibly he was exploring our breakfast remains
when a barrier of huge flies blessed his presence.
They were there to chronicle his competence.
He needed us: suddenly, that trans-stuff wouldn't do it.
But it was our hour for sheep-dumplin' tea.

They had Bates betwixt the windpipe and the lights.
His face looked like blackened embers.
And then he was bitten by a rabid mule.
The whole lot of us "aboriginals" sat sympathetic
through most of the show, Suzie was sniffling.

Bates had certainly botched up this one.
I snatched the whip from my surrogate's wife
and dimly felt an aromatic pellet enter my chilblains.
Skunk oil, that's what I need, a mess of peach roots.
The curving, scrawny scythe of my anger outwardly

surrendered to the merciful lichen camped idly
on our strange immortality. Which precipitated
a wound that could heal itself with a madstone.
My admiration for Bates was intense, intimate.
I peeped at him like a gamekeeper, I mentally clicked

the bushwa of his straw hat and glass bottles,
his cart of muffled gossip. If he remotely deviated,
if his blessed footage is inaccurate in any way,
are we less real? Goodbye, Bates, you sturdy fellow,
and goodbye, merry-go-round! We shall never meet again.

On the Chinese Painter/Poet
Wu Hui

He was unmistakably Chinese, his tongue
slanted and his stomach blushed.
There was a certain thickness to his method:
he would glue his materials to his body
for exactly 21 days prior to working,
and meditate exclusively upon criminal matters.
No phone calls, no music, only the tree frogs
which he had pinned to a polished apple. . . .

During that painful gestation period his mother
referred to him as "the inert seed." She dangled
her breast in front of his eyebrows and said,
"That's not my Son. Ink, all he thinks about
is ink."

And yet there was a blueprint on his hips,
his knees were strengthened with wood.
His neck was draped in a sublime, reddish paper,
his teeth were outlined in cardboard.
He was going some place venomous eventually.

Unless there is something he has overlooked.
Is he overcome by jealousy?
Unless his faith weakens at the moment of flowering,
he is besieged by errors, or his flair
turns on him, destructive, and a raven
is permitted to decide his fate.
Is he seldom comforted, is he compelled
and radiant, aroused and honest
and innocent of financial incentives?
He is.

When Wu Hui prepared to place the aureole
about the head of a divinity, silent crowds
gathered in awe to watch his flawless lightning swish.

And during the night he slept in a transparent coffin
made of glass.

The List of Famous Hats

Napoleon's hat is an obvious choice I guess to list as a famous hat, but that's not the hat I have in mind. That was his hat for show. I am thinking of his private bathing cap, which in all honesty wasn't much different than the one any jerk might buy at a corner drugstore now, except for two minor eccentricities. The first one isn't even funny: Simply it was a white rubber bathing cap, but too small. Napoleon led such a hectic life ever since his childhood, even farther back than that, that he never had a chance to buy a new bathing cap and still as a grown-up—well, he didn't really grow that much, but his head did: He was a pinhead at birth, and he used, until his death really, the same little tiny bathing cap that he was born in, and this meant that later it was very painful to him and gave him many headaches, as if he needed more. So, he had to vaseline his skull like crazy to even get the thing on. The second eccentricity was that it was a *tricorn* bathing cap. Scholars like to make a lot out of this, and it would be easy to do. My theory is simple-minded to be sure: that beneath his public head there was another head and it was a pyramid or something.

Made in Holland

Pigtails fiddles with my riverbed,
she shoots some plutonium up my harpsichord.
I am here in Holland up a nut tree.
I walk the shopping mall in my pajamas.
My cologne seems to intoxicate everyone.
Deluded cattle walk out of the barbershop
saying things like "Nice pajamas," and
"Didn't I see you at the golf club last week?"
"Alms," I say, "alms for the Sacred Rifles.
Alms for the Pampered Daughters of the Dragonfly."
Papa's up a nut tree in Holland, Pigtails
reposes over the fretwork of his dominion.
I am tethered to some daft subterfuge.
A doorbell rings, but there is no door.
Chuckle. A buzz, a bundle arrives:
someone in clogs is bringing it toward me.
It is my fever they want. I reach for the mop
and fall, fall quaintly against fluffy sashes,
and I fall on Pigtails, prod her
bereaved haven, skim the blemish of her starch.
And that is why I am in Holland.
That must be why, tulip.

Islands of Lunch

Red snapper with tabouli,
I tucked the napkin into my drink.
Smooching broke out at the next table.

I am talking a luncheon language
to a Lebanese architect
posing as a recently divorced Finn
in the Peachtree Center.

Red snapper, until the species
cannot afford summer vacations,
lunching on the bottom,
farming among the lower broccoli.

"I am a pagan, I will always be a pagan,"
a faculty wife explains. . . .

A determined waiter surfaces
with pastry fit for war.

"But Jim, I don't see how we
can afford to marry, I am just a poor
bookie who happens to be the sister
of Lawrence of Arabia, and you know

his insurance coverage wasn't that good."

Hurry Up and Wait

Until your hat floats,
until the roseola on your earlobes
permeates the cubicle of your thoughts.
And the bladderpods explode against your kneecaps
like amulets worn by addled aviators.
Hurry up and wait, I am that longshot warbler
with a clipboard, inspecting the dappled moments
the hours with their syllables like karate.
Until I see through my cottage like infrared,
O wan vermin! Your calisthenics in the creamery
move gumballs home to my delirium
where we are happy, where every fiber of our motto
is a smooth brunette released on a misdemeanor.
And while the calendars and clocks are aging quaintly,
I sponge the honeysuckle and spank the seismograph
for telling me lies (it is pastel and rather lumpy
as I write this). The Doctor has slipped me
some placebos, but there are thorns in them,
mundane thorns. Legions of still minutes
crest and fall—see, I am making a quilt of them,
a crazy quilt of all their floppy calamities,
persuasive in that, well, I am still here,
and they are dead, but in a kinetic sort of way.
So I hurry up and wait, until my hat floats,
until my calluses have captivated yours
and we are, at last, truly copacetic.

Hanging-out with Howard, Looking Around for Charmagne

If you ain't where you are
you're no place. Crazed
upon the wintry streets of

Amherst, Howard Dupuis and I
were sure we'd meet her around
the Happy Hour to slake. She

would make us feel better
about ourselves. Great is
the Night with its loaves

and parcels! Unless Enigma
be her name and all along
beside us. She kept our pace,

made her replies in silence.
The logic stiffened, our gestures
died, and we were curiosities

more beautiful, at last some
sense, so that the dream
diminished, ah, the loose chaos

of dreams, chessplaying with
the ethereal: *My late wife and I*
are going to become a father

because Mayor Daley is coming back
disguised as a bull-dyke
in an effort to infiltrate

our softball team! It is dark
and there are very few choices
left. The hands reaching out

shut down the Factory. So Rocky
died at his Aerobics class, some
kind of Hare Krishna hang-gliding.

Okay, Howard, let's call it quits.
Another night and our Divine Other
has slipped through our fingers,

mysteriously healing in her absence
the wound her absence brewed, O Love!

About the author

James Tate was born in Kansas City, Missouri, and grew up there. His first book, *The Lost Pilot,* won the Yale Series of Younger Poets award in 1967. Dudley Fitts, editor of the Yale Series at the time, wrote: "James Tate sounds to me like no one I have ever read— utterly confident, with an effortless elegance of control, in both diction and composition, that would be rare in a poet of any age and that is particularly impressive in a first book. I do not know who taught him to sing such songs. It is enough for me that he is singing them." Since then Tate has published eight other volumes of poetry: *The Oblivion Ha-Ha, Hints to Pilgrims, Absences, Hottentot Ossuary, Viper Jazz, Riven Doggeries, Constant Defender,* and *Reckoner.* He has lived for extended periods in Sweden, Ireland, and Spain, and in the United States has taught at the University of California, Berkeley, Columbia University, and the University of Massachusetts.

About the book

This book was typeset by G & S Typesetters, Inc. of Austin, Texas, in Meridien, was printed on 60-pound Miami Book Vellum paper by Arcata Kingsport, Inc. of Kingsport, Tennessee, and was bound by Arcata Kingsport. The design is by Joyce Kachergis Book Design and Production of Bynum, North Carolina.

Wesleyan University Press, 1986